Original title:
Lace and Longing

Copyright © 2025 Creative Arts Management OÜ
All rights reserved.

Author: Giselle Montgomery
ISBN HARDBACK: 978-1-80586-040-2
ISBN PAPERBACK: 978-1-80586-512-4

Remnants of Lost Touch

A thread unraveled on the floor,
Once held tight, now can't explore.
A sock now lost, where did it go?
With every step, I'm just a show.

The texture soft, but memory's rough,
Did we lose it all or just enough?
A fabric's role in stories told,
Can't help but chuckle at moments bold.

Veiled Wishes

In a drawer lies a tattered dream,
An odd confetti of wishes unseen.
With each fold, a giggle breaks free,
Who knew that fabric held such glee?

A patchwork quilt, the secrets hide,
Stitched together with laughter inside.
Each color shouts of silly delight,
A blanket of joy on a chilly night.

Silhouettes of Affection

A silhouette cast in schadenfreude,
Can't take seriously this love mode.
Two mismatched socks in a playful dance,
Custom fits are just a chance.

They twirl and swirl in a vivid array,
Misadventures lead them astray.
Yet here they twine, a comedic sight,
In mismatched glory, they take flight.

Echoes in Every Stitch

Every stitch a secret joke,
In laughter's grasp, we ensconce.
A sweater old, with tales to tell,
Of fashion flops, all's not that well.

Unraveled yarn, what a delight,
We wear our blunders, oh so tight!
In every loop, a belly laugh,
Life's silly threads make quite the craft.

Whispered Stitches

In the corner, threads take flight,
Poking fingers, what a sight!
Bobbins bouncing, dance around,
Whispers turn to laughter sound.

Needle's antics, full of glee,
Stitching stories, come and see!
Fabric tales that tickle our toes,
Hold the secrets that nobody knows.

Tapestries of Affection

Yarn cats tumble in playful chase,
While odd socks hold a secret place.
Every pattern, a tale we make,
From knots and loops, no hearts will break.

Patches sing of times we've shared,
With silly stitches that we dared.
Thread by thread, the laughter grows,
A tangled mess, but everybody knows.

Frayed Dreams

In a pile of dreams so tattered,
Undone seams, does it even matter?
Mismatched patches of hope and fun,
Chasing hearts until we run.

A button here, a ribbon there,
Life's a quilt, we sew with care.
But wait! What's this? A silly string,
Funny faces, joy they bring.

Woven Emotions

Knots of feelings, tight and loose,
Stitches rattle, let them loose!
Woven whims with every twirl,
Capturing laughter in a whirl.

Frayed edges, a colorful dance,
Threads go wild, they take a chance.
In patterns new, we find our way,
With giggles sewn in every sway.

Fabric of Time

In a closet, I found a sock,
Pondering if it was a rock.
It rolled in a dance, oh so spry,
Wishing it could learn to fly.

A button lost, in the depths of fate,
Hoping to find its perfect mate.
It's a mystery why they roam,
In the fabric of time, far from home.

The Weave of Whispers

A thread of tales, spun so tight,
Socks gossip in the dead of night.
Sweaters giggle in winter's chill,
While scarves plot, with slight thrill.

One sleeve's longing for a hug,
While the other is snug as a bug.
Amidst the stitches, secrets flow,
In the weave of whispers, no one will know.

Creases of the Heart

Ironing shirts with a heavy sigh,
Each crease tells a tale of why.
The tie, a joker with its knot,
Scarfs in the corner, feeling caught.

As I fold the past, it laughs,
A t-shirt teaching its brave staffs.
In each wrinkle, joy and pain,
A comical dance in the rain.

Fluttering Silks

Silks flit about like butterflies,
Chasing dreams under sunny skies.
A rogue hem that darts away,
Winking, "Come, let's dance and play!"

Chiffon whispers, "Catch me if you can!"
While denim sighs, "I'm the grounded man."
In a whirl of colors, they all prance,
Fluttering silks in a fabric dance.

Woven Dreams in Twilight

In twilight's glow, where fancies play,
A tangle of threads on a grand ballet.
A sock mismatched, yet bold in cheer,
Whispers of wishes, drawing near.

A caper untold, with stitches so spry,
Mocking the doves that flit through the sky.
With every knot, a giggle unfurled,
In the tapestry of this wobbly world.

Embraces of Gossamer

A web of wishes spun all around,
Catching the giggles that float on the ground.
Twirling like napkins in a cosmic ball,
Each flutter inviting, no hint of a fall.

Draped in delight, what a curious sight,
A grand escapade in the mellow moonlight.
Tickling the toes with a delicate tease,
In a dance of the breezes, life's sure to please.

The Echo of Silken Hues

Silken echoes in a playful refrain,
Dress-up dolls prance in the sun and the rain.
The fabric of laughter stretched oh so wide,
With giggles and whirls as dreams collide.

Colors collide in a riotous spree,
Chasing each other like friends at a spree.
Who thought that threads could dance and delight,
In the merry embrace of the starry night?

Patterns of the Heart

Patterns of life woven with care,
Life's a riddle, a jig, an affair.
Even the snags are part of the show,
A cheeky dance where silliness grows.

In every stitch, a quirky little plot,
A heart's desire wrapped in a knot.
Embracing the quirky with laughter's own tune,
Life's fabric is bright, under the smiling moon.

Surrendering to Shadows

In corners where secrets play,
My socks dance and fade away.
Ghostly whispers, silent peeps,
They tango while my closet sleeps.

With every creak, I spill my tea,
Spooky socks, come dance with me!
A phantom sip, a slippery slide,
Together we must take this ride.

Tender Webs of Emotion

Caught in a sticky, sweet delight,
My cat's tangled in yarn, what a sight!
Yearning for cuddles, without a care,
She pounces, her purrs float in the air.

A woolen ball, a ballad of fun,
My heart's a puppy, always on the run.
With yarn in the fray, our hearts entwine,
Two fuzzy souls, so absurdly divine.

Curled Petals and Unspoken Wishes

With petals curled in shades so bright,
I whisper dreams into the night.
But bees buzz back, oh, what a fuss,
"Your wish is mine, just ride the bus!"

A daisy's laugh, a tulip's tease,
I plant my dreams beneath the trees.
They giggle, sway, then hide away,
While I just stand here, hoping they stay.

The Lace of Memory

Memories flutter like butterflies,
Whimsical thoughts in pastel skies.
Each moment stitched, oh what a scene,
My grandma's quilt, it's quite the meme!

Patterns flash in joyful tune,
Unruly threads misbehave by noon.
Laughing echoes of days gone by,
Tangled stories that make me sigh.

Invisible Ribbons

In a drawer where secrets sleep,
Lie whispers tangled in a heap.
A sock's a friend, though it won't speak,
And dreams entwined, oh, so unique.

An apron dons its lively flair,
While mismatched buttons dance with care.
With every tug, a giggle stays,
As silly knots will knit their plays.

The jingle oh-so-random calls,
While kitchen chaos builds its walls.
A spatula slips, a whisk takes flight,
In comical jests beneath the light.

Our hearts all stitched in fitful seams,
With twine that holds our wacky dreams.
So let the humor rule the day,
In this fabric dance, let's sway away.

Tangled Devotion

A scarf that swirls around my neck,
Gets caught in doors, a perfect wreck.
It pulls me back, but I can't fight,
And laugh as I look out at the night.

My shoes can't seem to find their mates,
They trip me up in heated debates.
With every tread, they spin around,
In this merry mess, I'm glory-bound.

Necklaces twist like ballroom twirls,
A battle of beads that gives me swirls.
With every twist, my laughter grows,
At each mishap that life bestows.

Yet tangled charms and laugh-filled schemes,
Paint portraits bright of whimsy dreams.
In knots we find our silly grace,
And stumble through this tangled space.

Mimicry of Touch

Two fuzzy mittens play their role,
As I make snowballs, heart and soul.
They throw a fit, misplaced delight,
As snowy fluff takes off in flight.

A rubber chicken in my hand,
Jokes fly like seeds across the land.
With every squeeze, a chuckle bursts,
In silly antics, joy immerses.

And when the sun begins to set,
The shadows creep, and laughter's met.
A ticklish breeze across my cheek,
Brings funny memories, oh so meek.

So in this game of feel and fun,
With goofy smiles, we have just won.
A touch of humor lights the spark,
In this whimsical, joyous lark.

The Threaded Heart

A puppet's string ties laughs to woe,
As dance hall antics steal the show.
With stiffened arms, it sways and spins,
In awkward charm, the giggle wins.

A sock puppet's face, a grin so wide,
Echoes joys that never hide.
With every move in this charade,
Our happiness is hand-made.

The patchwork quilt grows tales so bold,
With snippets stitched in thread and gold.
Each quirky square holds memories bright,
In stitched-up dreams that bounce with light.

Our hearts are woven with a thread,
Of silly moments always spread.
So let's embrace this joyful art,
In every laughter, there beats a heart.

Chasing Threaded Moments

In a world of tangled strings,
I chase after everything.
The yarn keeps slipping away,
While my cat laughs at my play.

Needles poke and scissors tease,
Crafting joy with perfect ease.
Each stitch tells a silly tale,
Of epic fails that never pale.

Fabric soft as dreams so bright,
Yet I trip in fabric's light.
Sewing circles round the floor,
And landing near the open door.

With each twist, a giggle grows,
As I fumble, oh, how it shows!
Chasing threads, I weave my fate,
In a knit-pick mess that's never late.

Ethereal Caresses

A feather's touch makes everyone smile,
My soft embrace is a playful style.
In clouds of tulle, I prance and twirl,
Spinning around like a silly girl.

Phantom fibers float through the air,
Tickling noses, oh, how unfair!
With laughter echoing in my wake,
I dance in whispers, make no mistake.

In whimsical worlds of gentle threads,
I dream of frolics, of lightweight beds.
Each blush of fabric, a cheeky tease,
While I lose my pants and fall to my knees.

Elegance dances on the breeze,
With tangled skeins that never please.
Yet in this chaos, joy does glide,
In a silly swirl, I take it in stride.

Intersections of Desire

At every crossroad, I take a chance,
Patching dreams in a silly dance.
Bobbins spin, and troubles twine,
As I sew my heart, oh, so divine.

Threads of fate pull at my seams,
In this patchwork quilt of silly dreams.
Each button picked, I wear with pride,
In garments of laughter, I shall abide.

I stumbled once upon a heart,
It rolled away, what a funny start!
In this fabric store of laughter's chase,
Patterns collide in a joyful space.

So here I stand with tangled grace,
In the fabric of wishes, I find my place.
Stitch by stitch, I mend and create,
A tapestry woven of joyful fate.

Stitching the Soul

I sew buttons onto my heart,
In a patchwork scheme, I play the part.
With wobbly lines and crooked seams,
I craft my life from fuzzy dreams.

Doodles on fabric, whimsical delight,
Giggles burst forth in the dead of night.
Every stitch, a little jest,
As I figure out how to look my best.

Snipping away at the threads of doubt,
With each snip, I dance and shout.
My soul's a quilt of funny quirks,
In this world of fabric, creativity lurks.

Patterns emerge from the chaos inside,
Sailing through moments on a colorful ride.
As I thread my needle and take my toll,
With every stitch, I stitch my soul.

The Dance of Fine Fibers

In the cupboard, they twirl and sway,
Resilient threads in a bright cabaret.
Twisted fortunes in cotton spin,
Waiting for someone to let them begin.

Feathers and frills, oh, what a sight,
Socks that dance in the quiet night.
They laugh at the hangers, all dull and gray,
Swaying and winking like it's their play.

A curtain that whispers, a frock on a spree,
Balloons of fabric, feeling so free.
Yet one's a disaster, it's mismatched and torn,
The joy of stitching, with threads all worn.

A coat with a sparkle, it steps on the scene,
Feigning its charm, oh so serene.
Yet inside it crinkles, a tale of its own,
In the mishmash of fibers, a dance is grown.

Patterns of Unfulfilled Desire

In drawers, they languish, in patterns untold,
A dream of soirees where glamour unfolds.
A polka dot beauty, she sighs with a glance,
While stripes call for joy in a whimsical dance.

A patchwork of wishes, they cheerfully sigh,
"I'll be worn someday, oh so spry!"
Yet here they all sit, a colorful mess,
Plotting their fortunes, rehearsing success.

The gloves are jealous, they cackle and mock,
"What about us? We're quite the nice flock!"
But who needs a pair when you've got a lone?
A single sock giggles, defiantly grown.

Frills of regret hang in silence so thick,
A tapestry of hopes that just wouldn't stick.
But laughter emerges from frays and from tears,
In patterns of hope, we dance through our fears.

Threads of Hope and Sorrow

A needle's sharp jest, a thread's soft embrace,
In the guise of stitching, what a charming place.
One meets destiny while others get lost,
In the fabric of fate, oh, what a cost.

Mismatched buttons, the perfect delight,
They giggle and jiggle in the pale moonlight.
A tale of adventure in every wrong seam,
Forgotten from stories, yet somehow they beam.

With stitches of laughter, and seams of despair,
We wear them with pride, these signs we all share.
Each fabric's a memory, each fold is a laugh,
In a world made of fibers, we find our own path.

Through threads that entwine, both joy and dismay,
We twirl through the chaos at the end of the day.
In knots of confusion, there's humor, I swear,
For nothing complements a smile like a snare.

Woven Whispers in the Night

When shadows are cast, and the world fades away,
Threads start to mingle, and laughter will play.
A sheet like a blanket wraps secrets so tight,
In the weave of the evening, a tickle of light.

A scarf tells a joke, but we're still getting cold,
While a bonnet insists it's worth its own gold.
Yet hats are quite picky, a crown with disdain,
Sewing up tales of fashion's odd game.

Under the moon, those fibers come alive,
Woven whispers teasing, oh how they contrive.
A tapestry's waiting, with patterns so bright,
In a snicker of fate, we cherish the night.

Yet every old thread has a story to share,
With laughter and joy hidden deep in their glare.
So come dance with the fabric, let the mischief abound,
In the weave of old fibers, life's humor is found.

Threads of Desire

In a shop filled with frills, oh what a sight,
I tripped on a spool that rolled out of sight.
Stitching my dreams with a needle so keen,
Trying on hope, looking slim and serene.

A button pops off, what a comical fate,
"Is it my charm, or just an old plate?"
Fabric swirls dance in humor and cheer,
Cotton candy thoughts, I crave them near.

Whispering Delicacies

A silk scarf whispers secrets so sweet,
As I trip on the hem of my own two feet.
Chiffon dreams float through the air so bold,
Wishing for cupcakes instead of this gold.

Threads of mischief twirl round my waist,
"Do you think I'm stylish, or just misplaced?"
Nervous little giggles in every fine stitch,
Finding my way through a fashionable glitch.

Tangles of Yearning

My hair's a wild forest, a knotty surprise,
With ribbons and bows that dare to arise.
Hoping for neatness in a world overspun,
But my chaotic crown is just too much fun.

I crafted a dream, with sequins a-glow,
Yet tripping on fabric made me the show.
A mess of emotions, with giggles on cue,
Patching my heart with a clumsy debut.

Fragile Bonds of Heart

In a teacup of moments, I find my delight,
With fragile connections that sparkle so bright.
Knotted together like a shoestring gone mad,
I laugh at the mess, not a bit feeling sad.

Dancing with joy, in a fabric of play,
Wearing my heart on my sleeve every day.
Even when tangled, my spirit won't part,
These threads, my dear friend, are the song of my heart.

Unraveled Hearts

In the closet, secrets twirl,
Mismatched socks start to swirl,
A tangled mess of styles grand,
I swear they danced, hand in hand.

Oh, the scars from yesterday's fun,
Ribbons tied, but not quite done,
Chasing dreams in threads so bright,
Who knew knots could feel so right?

With every twist, the giggles roll,
Fashion faux pas, a comical sole,
Threads of laughter wrapped so tight,
Could this be love at first sight?

So here we are, a whimsical bunch,
Stitching stories, laughing at lunch,
In this mess, our hearts will find,
The joy that ties us, sweetly kind.

Soft Patterns of Memory

Faded florals in my mind,
Whirling whimsies, now unlined,
Each memory a dainty thread,
Tickles of romance, lightly spread.

Cupcakes frosted, just like fate,
Sprinkles flew, a messy slate,
Flirting with the baker's grin,
Sugar highs, where love begins.

In a patchwork quilt so grand,
We stitched our dreams with silly hands,
Hold my heart, oh what a tease,
Laughter woven with such ease.

Time unravels, yet we cling,
To the joy that memories bring,
In soft patterns, we will dance,
Mixing colors, a silly chance.

Echoes of Embrace

A clumsy hug, two hearts collide,
Bumbling dreams we cannot hide,
In the echoes laugh we share,
Socks and kisses everywhere.

Silly moments, like bouncing balls,
We trip and stumble through the halls,
Woven tightly with a grin,
Do we fall, or do we spin?

A sprinkle here, a twirl so wide,
In this dance, we take the ride,
Holding tightly to the jest,
In the chaos, we feel blessed.

With every slip and silly sway,
We create our own ballet,
In this whirl, the laughter blooms,
Soft melodies in crowded rooms.

Fragile Connections

Paper cups and silly strings,
Tangled chats, the joy it brings,
With every word, a silly thread,
Building up what's lightly said.

Cups of warmth and playful smiles,
Woven tales from distant miles,
Whispers shared like tiny birds,
In every laugh, no need for words.

Frayed edges but hearts so bright,
We dance through days, holding tight,
Wobbly seats and coffee spills,
Through every laugh, affection thrills.

In this tapestry of fun,
There's a bond that we've begun,
Fragile threads, yet so profound,
In laughter's arms, forever bound.

Elusive Connections in Silken Time

In a world of tangled threads,
A sock in search of a mate.
Lost in soft, twinkling dance,
The clock giggles—I'm late!

Windows whisper tales of flirt,
With curtains swaying wide.
A breeze brings whispers of dessert,
As feelings try to hide.

Cocktails spill upon the floor,
As hearts break into song.
The punchline's just around the door,
Where laughter won't take long.

But just when I think I see,
A shape that might be mine.
It slips away, mischievous glee,
Leaving echoes, sweet and fine.

Hidden Pathways of the Heart

In those hallways of our dreams,
I tripped on longing's shoe.
Caught in shadows of moonbeams,
A dance partner—who knew?

Giggles echo off the walls,
As jesters steal the show.
My heart leaps—oh, the stalls!
Where all the heartstrings flow.

Maps of love with lines so curvy,
Lead to places most absurd.
Finding treasures, feeling swervy,
As shy birds sing their word.

But oh, these paths are quite the maze,
With giggles as my guide.
I'll follow fate's elusive ways,
On this merry-hearted ride.

Threads of Desire

Stitch by stitch, I weave my dreams,
In patterns bold and bright.
Hoping that the sunlight beams,
Upon a love at night.

But every twist is full of fun,
Like spaghetti on the floor.
A dance that's never quite been done,
Leaving hearts to explore.

Embroidery of laughter drips,
As threads unravel slow.
Each knot a tale of silly quips,
That only we could know.

Yet when I think I have it right,
My needle finds a snag.
A joyful fool beneath the light,
With love—a quirky brag.

Veils of Yearning

Whispers wrapped in softest pride,
The fabric hides a jest.
Beneath the layers, smiles collide,
In every silly quest.

Veils that flutter with a tease,
As secrets try to bloom.
I dance to tunes of breeze,
My heart? A real cartoon!

Peeking out from hidden folds,
A wink that tends to sway.
In tangled cloth, my story unfolds,
As quirky dreams lead the way.

But just when I think I can see,
The fabric's pulled away!
I laugh and shout, "Oh, let me be!"
In this game we play.

Bound by Soft Whispers

In the draw of a thread, I start to conspire,
With wigs on the floor, it's my new attire.
Stitching my dreams under layers of fluff,
While laughing at patterns, thinking this is enough.

A tangled-up dance with a needle, I dive,
Creating a chaos where giggles arrive.
Patterns are tricky, they twist and they tie,
But oh, what a fuss when I think I can fly!

Threading my heart with a wink and a grin,
I wear all my hopes, like a jester's new skin.
In a world full of frills, it's hard to stay grounded,
Yet each little twist leaves me utterly astounded.

So cheers to the moments, the stitches and flips,
In this whimsical waltz, let's take all the trips.
With a misstep or two, and a snip here and there,
We'll twirl through the fabric, with laughter to share.

In the Tapestry of You

Where threads intertwine in a mischief-filled spree,
I tangle my heart in decorative glee.
With each playful knot, I smirk and I sigh,
As the fabric of friendship tries hard to fly.

You thread me with stories that loop and that spin,
Sewing laughs from memories stitched carefully in.
The colors might clash, but it's all in good fun,
As we quilt up the night, under bright summer sun.

I'm prancing around in this patchwork delight,
With fringes and sequins that shimmer so bright.
Accidental splashes leave patterns awry,
Yet the joy in the making makes my spirits fly.

So here's to our weaving, so silly and bold,
Tales stitched in laughter, never to grow old.
In this goofy creation, it's all about you,
The stitches we cherish, with threads that run true.

Veils of Unseen Affection

A bustling bazaar of bright patterned puffs,
Where affection's tucked under some silken fluff.
I trip over sentiments veiled in a dance,
But it's hard not to laugh at this hapless romance.

With each twist and turn, the fabric's alive,
Whispering quirks as we jive and we thrive.
The hidden emotions peek out from the seams,
Playing hide and seek through our extravagant dreams.

Cloaked in hilarity, I wrap up my hope,
In puffs that are silly, yet help me to cope.
A tumble of glamour, a swirl of delight,
And I giggle at feelings that flutter through the night.

So here's to the veils, all frilly and funny,
In the grandeur of moments, honey-sweet and sunny.
We'll dance through the chaos, unthreaded yet true,
In a tapestry woven with all shades of you.

Stitches of the Past

Oh, the tales that are woven from twine and from thread,
Like a scrapbook of giggles where mischief was spread.
Each stitch is a memory, a snicker, a sigh,
Reminding me fondly of moments gone by.

In knots of nostalgia, I seam up my heart,
As I chuckle at times when we stumbled and part.
The patterns keep shifting, but laughter stays bright,
As the fabric of friendship surrounds us at night.

With quips from the past that rise like the sun,
We stitch in the colors of all the good fun.
These threads tell our story, all tangled and spun,
And in each silly twirl, I'll always have won.

Though patches may fade, and some seams may wear thin,

The joy of the journey, with you, I begin.
For every lighthearted memory we cast,
Is a stitch in the fabric that shadows the past.

Veiled Aspirations

In a tangle of threads, quite absurd,
Stitching dreams that seem to be blurred.
A ribbon that wiggles, a bow that won't sit,
Dancing to melodies, just a tad off wit.

A veil of intentions, wrapped like a snack,
Hoping for glory, not a fashion flack.
A twirl and a whirl, oh what a delight,
Lost in the fraying, it feels just right.

Ponder the choices, all crumpled in haste,
One thread leads to laughter, another to waste.
But oh, what a joy when they finally meet,
A party of patterns, oh isn't that neat?

So here's to the threads, both tangled and true,
In the fabric of hopes, we bid you adieu.
With giggles and grins, we stitch and we spin,
In the quest for the perfect, let the madness begin!

Dreams in the Weave

In a world where threads conspire,
Bobbins dance as hearts retire.
Twists and turns in every seam,
Stitching laughter, love's bright dream.

A tangled mess of yarn and cheer,
Knots that giggle, never fear.
Patterns shift, the colors clash,
Who needs rules? We'll make a splash!

Each fabric tear a silly tale,
Of mismatched socks that always fail.
Sewing kits, they sprout a grin,
As scissors snip—let chaos win!

Through patches bright and frayed-out seams,
We weave the fabric of our dreams.
In every stitch, a funny flair,
A joyous mess beyond compare.

Caresses of the Past

Whispers linger in the seams,
Once a dress now full of dreams.
Oh, the parties it once wore,
Now a bag that holds some more!

Each button tale, a jest we share,
Threads of laughter fill the air.
Mismatched gloves come out to play,
Waving 'hello' in a quirky way!

Faded patterns, once so bold,
Laughing at the tales they're told.
Every tear a magical twist,
In this fabric, joy can't be missed!

So remember that old wooly hat,
With ears that flop and fight the cat.
These woven relics hold us tight,
Caressing memories, pure delight.

Tied by Time

Clocks keep ticking in a flick,
Socks have vanished—what a trick!
Time unraveled, threads bemused,
Timing's just a game we've used.

Chasing fabric through the years,
Laughter mingles with the tears.
Worn-out seams and crooked lines,
In this web, the humor shines.

Caught in zippers, stuck in seams,
Life's a patchwork of our dreams.
With every thread, a moment's fun,
Tick-tock, tick-tock, we're all undone!

Yet in this chaos, we find grace,
A quirky smile upon each face.
Warp and weft, a dance sublime,
Together we are taught by time.

The Fabric of Dreams

In threads of mischief we delight,
Puppy paws in fabric fight.
Quilts of laughter, hugs abound,
Stitching joy from all around.

Uneven hems and bobbles bold,
Each mishap, a story told.
Colorful patches, here they sing,
Even buttons join the fling!

We patch our lives with bits and scraps,
As summer sun and winter snaps.
Frayed edges tell of times long gone,
Yet in this mess, we carry on.

So here's to fabric woven tight,
With silly dreams and sheer delight.
In every fold and twist we trust,
To laugh at life is surely a must.

Silk and Secrets

In the closet, chaos reigns,
Threads twirl like playful trains.
I search for that elusive dress,
But find only socks in a mess.

Buttons giggle, seams sigh loud,
Wishing they could join the crowd.
In this fabric realm of glee,
Is that a sweater mocking me?

I pull at strands, they dance away,
Textiles tease in a quirky sway.
Oh, the treasures that lurk within,
A shy scarf dodging the chin spin.

A hat pops up, with a wink and grin,
"Try me on, let the fun begin!"
But as I wear this wobbly thing,
Who knew socks could lead to spring?

Entwined Echoes

A scarf whispers secrets near,
Tales of laughter, bits of cheer.
In the tangled threads, they hide,
Like a kitten bound with pride.

Oh the patterns, wild and bright,
Try to match them, what a sight!
Stripes and polka dots collide,
Like my hopes when I can't decide.

I twirl in skirts that twist and shout,
Each step sparks a little doubt.
Is that a patch? Or just my luck?
How did I end up so... unstuck?

Mirrors crack with laughter lines,
Fabric flutters, crossing signs.
In the echoes, joy and mess,
I embrace this lovely stress.

The Art of Unraveling

A spool of thread spills on the floor,
A winding road I must explore.
Each loop and knot a puzzle set,
Who knew chaotic could be pet?

Tangles tease and coils complain,
Like my cat in the falling rain.
She pounces on the rolling threads,
While I just trip and see red.

Pants that fit? A dream, it seems,
Always snatching fabric dreams.
Yet in the fray, I laugh so loud,
For give or take, I'm joyful, proud.

A stitch here, a stitch there,
Who knew creating could be wear?
With every twist, I come undone,
Yet still, it feels like such good fun.

Yearning in the Fabric

In a world where denim reigns,
I fall for velvet, soft and vain.
A quest for comfort, style, and flair,
In thrift shop treasures, I find my prayer.

Fabrics chat like old dear friends,
Each fold and crease, a story sends.
Am I too bold? Or quite the dandy?
Perhaps these stripes are just a handy.

One sock goes rogue, and starts to flee,
The other waits, perplexed, you see.
I chase after it, a silly race,
Who knew that laundry had such grace?

In the end, it's all in jest,
Fabric dreams put to the test.
In this textile world, I gleefully play,
For who said fashion can't be a ballet?

Texture of Memories

In a drawer of dreams, old socks lie,
Crumpled reminders of times gone by.
Each stitch a jest, a wink from fate,
Comical tales weave, never too late.

Nostalgic flings with buttons lost,
My grandma's knitting, a curious cost.
Yarns tangled like stories, absurd and bright,
We laugh at the chaos, oh what a sight!

Colors collide in wild dismay,
Sweaters knitted in odd shades of gray.
Each fabric a rebel, a story untold,
In mismatched patterns, memories unfold.

With every tug, a chuckle and cheer,
Stitches that shout, "How'd we end up here!"
Life's fuzzy whims and fabric so bold,
In each playful thread, joys manifold.

Wistful Weavings

In mom's old quilt, secrets reside,
The stitches are tales of laughter and pride.
Patterns unravel with each cozy night,
Tickled with dreams, under soft moonlight.

Afternoon picnics with ice cream spills,
Threads of adventure, and nimble thrills.
With every tear, a new patch goes in,
"Oops! That's a memory" wrapped in a grin.

A hat that was worn through sunshine and rain,
Odd little buttons that squabble like bane.
Each fabric a footnote in life's great book,
We wink at the fashion, give fate a look.

So let the fabric of life intertwine,
In each little seam, there's more than just time.
With giggles and twirls, we dance through the day,
In whimsical weavings, we laugh and play.

Shadows of Silk

Through the shimmer, a story is spun,
Silhouettes prance in the warmth of the sun.
Capes made of daydreams, oh what a sight,
Breezy laughter that flutters in flight.

A scarf by the coffee, a rogue little tale,
Stolen from closets, never to pale.
"Who wore it better?" we playfully muse,
In shadows of silk, there's never a snooze.

Buried in ruffles, the laughter ignites,
Frills of mischief that conquer the nights.
With each sassy thread, we strut down the lane,
Giggling echoes in fabric remain.

Hey, look at that spark! A dress of pure jest,
Dancing in colors, it's life's odd quest.
With stitches so silly, we twirl and we swing,
In shadows of silk, what joy do we bring!

Patterns in the Wind

The breeze carries whispers of threads yet to weave,
Witty little tales, if only you believe.
Dancing in patterns, the leaves spun with glee,
They chuckle at shadows while laughing at me.

Breezy encounters with shirts hanging low,
Who knew they'd witness such a colorful show?
Twirling like tops, our garments take flight,
In whimsical patterns, we bask in delight.

Frayed ends and knits, a riotous mess,
Kick off your shoes, let spontaneity bless.
We spin and we swirl through the garden of fate,
Where laughter's the fabric and joy is the rate.

So fly with the fabrics that flutter and sway,
Embrace every quirk, let fun lead the way.
In the patterns we find in the whispering wind,
Life's quirky designs surely provoke a grin!

Faded Fragments

In the drawer, a tangled mess,
Missing pieces, oh what a guess!
Colors bright, now dull and shy,
A craft gone wrong, oh me, oh my!

A thread that runs a wild spree,
Hiding secrets, just wait and see!
Knots that giggle, loops that squirm,
Every pull makes the fabric worm!

Sewing dreams with a bumpy stitch,
Got my hopes up, then they hitch!
A tapestry of giggles alone,
Who needs magic when you've grown?

So gather the bits, let's have some fun,
In this fabric, laughter's begun!
With each mishap, a tale unfolds,
In this patch, my heart it holds!

Currents of Affection

A tangled web of thoughts so sweet,
Like dancers in a chaotic beat!
Threads that spark, a playful dive,
Crafty hearts, all come alive!

Swirls of color, a whirl and a twirl,
Oh what a mix in this quirky world!
Stitch by stitch, we weave our fate,
Jokes sewn tight as we celebrate!

Wobbly seams, but we still cheer,
Each fabric flaw brings laughter near!
Patchwork dreams, a twist and twine,
Together we make the silliest design!

So raise a toast to our bright creation,
A splendid blend of jovial elation!
In every snag, a giggle stays,
Embroidery of silly ways!

Embroidered Whispers

In the quiet, whispers stitch,
Funny tales that make us twitch!
With every knot, laughter in bloom,
Who knew fabric could hold such room?

Stitching secrets with a sly grin,
Each little thread, a mischief within!
A snip here, a tuck over there,
In this quilt, we craft a flare!

Twirls and swirls, a riot of hue,
Every patch screams, 'Look at you!'
With needle and thread, we form a bond,
In this quilt, our stories respond!

So let's gather these giggly seams,
And stitch together all our dreams!
With each tiny loop, we make it right,
In the fabric of life, we shine bright!

The Art of Unraveling

Oh dear me, what a tangled sight,
Unraveling threads, a comedic fright!
Each little loop a twist of fate,
Trying to sew, but isn't it great?

Yarns unravel, with a funny dance,
Caught in stitches, a jesty prance!
Who needs order when chaos reigns?
In these knots, humor remains!

Laughter echoes with each tug,
A playful nudge, a woolly shrug!
My heart is stitched with yarn so bright,
In the mess, we find delight!

So here's to threads that lose their way,
In our hearts, they surely stay!
With each mishap, we revel and sing,
In this art of life, we find our bling!

The Touch of Fleeting Threads

In the corner, a sock lies lost,
Its partner is off on a wild cost.
Hoping their reunion's a success,
As laundromats hold fabric express.

The needle dances with grace so sly,
Stitching tales as the seams comply.
While buttons witness with a wink,
And thread whispers secrets, don't you think?

A scarf sways, but it's a bit too long,
Trips over feet as it hums a song.
It gives a twirl, but oh what a mess,
Yet laughter finds a way to impress.

Finding humor in tangled yarn,
We share a giggle over a charm.
For in the threads, we weave our cheer,
Making memories year by year.

Embroidered Dreams at Dawn

A quilt of colors lies on the floor,
Each patch with a story we can't ignore.
But one corner's flipped, what a sight,
It looks like a cat had a wild night!

Stitches crossed like words unspoken,
In the glow of morning, not a thread's broken.
Pillow fights erupt, feathers in flight,
As dreams unravel, oh what a delight!

A thimble rolls, with a cheeky grin,
As if to say, 'Let the fun begin!'
A tapestry of giggles we sew,
In daylight's glow, our chaos will grow.

So let the fabric tell our tale,
In laughter and joy, we will not fail.
For woven moments are what we keep,
With humor stitched in, we'll never sleep.

Hints of Melancholy

A thread hangs low, feeling a bit blue,
Caught in a web of 'what if' anew.
A crooked seam with tales to share,
But who would listen? Does anyone care?

In the attic, a vintage dress sighs,
Recalling nights under starry skies.
A pocket of dreams, now faded and worn,
Echoes of laughter, now tattered and torn.

A lonely button rolls out of view,
Hoping to find its mate—what to do?
But each tiny chuckle softens the plight,
As a wobbly stitch finds its courage to fight.

So let the shadows tease the thread's grace,
With a wink and a smile, we embrace the space.
Each weave, a reminder, life's tangled fun,
In wistful moments, laughter's never done.

Heartstrings in the Dark

The yarn ball bounces with silly flair,
While shadows twirl in the evening air.
A crafty mix of humor and scares,
Weaving tales of love that nobody shares.

With each knot tied tighter than before,
Hiding secrets that we can't ignore.
But in the dim light, it starts to gleam,
As laughter erupts, bursting the seam.

A hook and a loop make quite a pair,
Pulling together with a whimsical dare.
As heartstrings play a melody sweet,
In this fabric dance, we find our beat.

So we stitch away through the shades of the night,
Finding joy in the chaos, a flickering light.
For even in darkness, laughter shall spark,
With threads of delight, we conquer the dark.

Whispers of the Past

In a drawer, secrets reside,
A sock with holes, my heart's my guide.
Crumbs from cookies, oh what a mess,
Stitched up dreams in old velvet dress.

The cat in a hat, what a sight to see,
Waltzing with shadows, oh dearie me!
A tap of the foot, and an old record spins,
Lost in the laughter where youth begins.

Dining on pickles, a whimsical feast,
Juggling good times, never a least.
In kitchens of chaos, we twirl like a swirl,
Chasing the giggles, with a twinkle and whirl.

So here's to the quirks, we celebrate loud,
In slippers and socks, we stand oh so proud.
For moments we treasure, with love sewn tight,
In fabrics of memories, all feels so right.

Hidden Yearnings

Beneath the surface, a tickle of dreams,
An umbrella that giggles; it often seems.
Cakes with too much icing, quite the delight,
With sprinkles like stars on a whimsical night.

In a garden of wishes, the gnomes throw shade,
Watering whispers, in sunshine they wade.
Two socks on the line, a dance for the birds,
Hats worn backwards, we're favorites, absurd!

Carefree the moments we sprinkle with glee,
Hot air balloons floating, come fly with me!
We chase after rainbows, or puddles to jump,
In revelry's laughter, we bounce and we thump.

So here's our confession, oh what a treat,
In the circus of life, we dance on our feet.
With quips so delightful, we savor the play,
In patchwork of silliness, come laugh, let's stay.

Dusk of Emotions

As daylight fades, the silliness sings,
Of worn-out shoes and imaginary things.
Balloons in the sky, they're slipping away,
Like dreams in a tangle that choose not to stay.

The ice cream drips down, it's a race for the cone,
With giggles and sprinkles we make it our own.
Shoelaces tied up, in knots of delight,
A jester of fate, painting the night.

Clouds shape some laughter, we invent our own myth,
With echoes of joy, we forget and we whiff.
In twilight's embrace, the shenanigans blend,
Lost in the frolic, we bend and we mend.

So let's wrap our tales in the dusk's gentle weave,
For mischief and banter are all we believe.
With a wink and a grin, we toast to our cheer,
In the fading of daylight, our laughter we steer.

Softly Intertwined

Two mismatched socks share a secretive glance,
In the dance of the laundry, they find their romance.
A cat on the windowsill, plotting a scheme,
These whimsies of life feel like one big dream.

Cotton candy clouds float in stories we tell,
With bubbles and giggles, we laugh oh so well.
In the warmth of the kitchen, where chaos unfolds,
The mixing of flavors, a joy to behold.

Tickles of sunshine play on cheeky grins,
Where laughter erupts, our adventure begins.
In basket of laundry, the oddest of pairs,
We pull out the joy, forgetting our cares.

So let's bind the moments, with thread of delight,
In patchwork of stories, we weave through the night.
With twirls and with giggles, our journey's entwined,
In the fabric of memories, love's gently defined.

Intricate Hopes

In a world where threads collide,
I sought patterns none could hide.
My dreams, they danced on quirky lines,
Like mismatched socks in grand designs.

With laughter stitched in every seam,
I sat and pondered what could gleam.
A fortune found in tangled yarn,
Was it a joke, or just my charm?

Threads of futures spun so wide,
Between the giggles, I'd abide.
With every twist, a chuckle's breeze,
Who knew threads could tease with ease?

So I'll embrace this fabric life,
Where every knot can spark some strife.
In whimsical weaves of every hue,
I find my joy, how 'bout you?

Embracing the Unseen

Beneath the layers, joys do play,
Where shadows prance and mischief sway.
Invisible whims in a fabric so thin,
Whispering giggles where dreams begin.

A frolic of fibers with hopes untold,
To dance with jest under threads of gold.
Every stitch a story, comedic at best,
In the realm of the unseen, we jest.

Engaging the laughter that hides in the seams,
I find my delight in outlandish dreams.
Contrived moments that suddenly spark,
A surprise in the dark—a quip in the park!

So here's to the fabric that holds our glee,
Invisible wonders, oh can't you see?
With giggles woven in time's gentle loom,
Embracing the charm where laughter can bloom.

Tying the Past

Tethered memories, in knots they lie,
Mislaid moments that flutter and fly.
Each loop a chuckle, each twist a tease,
Binding the past with whimsical ease.

Old photos curled like candy wrappers sweet,
Hold stories wrapped in nostalgic heat.
Knots of the past, a humorous sight,
As I untangle, I chuckle with delight.

The more I pull, the more they sing,
Conversing memories, oh what a fling!
Like socks that vanish in laundry's embrace,
I laugh at the chase, the absurdity's grace.

So with every tie that I've ever spun,
I dance with the awkward, I laugh and run.
In this yarn of life, I weave and I play,
Tying the past in a funny ballet.

Weaving Through Midnight

As the clock ticks on, the threads intertwine,
Whimsical whispers become my design.
At midnight's door, humor's my guide,
Through shadows and fibers, I glide.

With a needle of laughter, I stitch the night,
Crafting a quilt of odd delight.
Each patch a giggle, each seam a grin,
In the fabric of dreams, my fun begins.

Spinning tales of the outright absurd,
In the quiet of midnight, dreams are stirred.
With every loop, I'm lost in a jest,
A spree of mischief, oh what a quest!

So let the moon watch over my spree,
As I weave through the night, wild and free.
In laughter's embrace, I'll find my thread,
Crafting a tapestry of joy instead.

Threads of Yesterday

In the closet, a tangle so bright,
Last season's hopes, lost in the light.
Twirls of fabric, jokes on the floor,
Why do I keep what I cannot ignore?

A dress too small, hangs like a tease,
Each stitch a memory, it's meant to please.
My waistline laughs, what's it got to say?
'Just one more cookie, come on, let's play!'

Buttons that wink, with mischief afoot,
As patterns tremble, it's getting quite cute.
With every fold, a giggle might sprout,
Yet here I am, still sorting it out.

On a rainy day, I'll tread with delight,
Sewing hopes in stitches, a humorous sight.
Who knew my blunders could shine so bold?
Threads of yesterday, both funny and old.

Sighs in the Stitch

A needle's dance, a scandalous spin,
Each tug and pull, let the chaos begin.
Fabric sighs, it knows what I'll try,
To stitch up my plans, yet I'm not that spry.

Twisting and turning, I frolic with thread,
Whispers of fabric fill dreams in my head.
"Oh look, a dart!" I'll cheerfully shout,
But who will fix this if I mess it out?

Stray threads giggle, they're plotting a tease,
Making a dress that's destined to seize.
Yet as I toil, with laughter I stitch,
Magic happens, isn't life a glitch?

So here I sit, with my crafty dreams,
A wardrobe of wonders, or so it seems.
Sighs in each stitch, but oh what a game,
For laughter's the fabric that drives me insane.

Elusive Patterns

Patterns on paper, a riddle unclear,
I trace and I plot, but what's my career?
Each curve is a mystery, tricks in disguise,
Like baking a cake that's just made of lies.

Sewing is simple, so I've been told,
But why can't I find that elusive fold?
As seams become monsters, they start to betray,
'Hey you, dear fabric, don't run away!'

Threads throw a party, and I'm running late,
Every stitch a chance, though none seem to mate.
Hems that unwind, like a tale unexpectedly,
I laugh at the chaos, so absurdly free.

So dare I embrace this whimsical dance?
With scissors a'cutting, I'm trapped in this trance.
Elusive, yet charming, this crafting spree,
Each cut a new chance to set fabric free!

Daring to Dream

In my studio, fabric whispers so bright,
'Dare to create, let the colors ignite!'
With scissors in hand, I dream up my fate,
Oh fabric, my muse, you're never too late.

Threading the needle, oh what a game,
Can the zigzag dance frame all my shame?
I stitch and I giggle, mistakes make me bold,
Who knew crafting could turn into gold?

Each piece I create has a life of its own,
Like cats on a mission, a vibe has been sown.
Patterns collide in a whimsical whirl,
It seems I'm embroidering my own little world.

So here's to the seams and the joys that they bring,
In a fabric of laughter, I'll learn how to swing.
Daring to dream in a stitchy delight,
Crafting a future that's quirky and bright!

Delicate Hues of Want

In a closet so bright, with colors that glow,
Ribbons and frills join the whimsical show.
A sock with a flair, the left one is grand,
The right one is missing, oh where did it land?

Buttons and bows dance in playful delight,
Each garment a story, each thread out of sight.
The shirt with a collar that thinks it can sing,
Yet always trips over its own precious bling.

Pants that are snug like a hug made of cheese,
They giggle and wiggle while teasing the knees.
A skirt with a twirl that wants to be free,
But dreads the disaster of a gust from the sea.

So here in the wardrobe, the fabrics conspire,
To weave all the moments that never expire.
With whimsy and charm, they tease and they play,
In the delicate hues of our closet ballet.

Craving in Silk

Oh, the softness that whispers, a tickle on skin,
A silk scarf that dances as dreams pull you in.
Ties itself tightly, now why is it shy?
It covers my sneeze, but does not lull my sigh.

Frilly delight on an apron that's bold,
Spills flour and sugar like a story retold.
Each ruffle a giggle, each flap has a voice,
It argues with sleeves, it just has no choice.

A waistcoat of charm, but its buttons conspire,
To pop one by one, as if playing with fire.
Tails of the jacket flick, flap, and they swish,
While I aim to impress; who grants me this wish?

So in the soft shine of a silken embrace,
We chase after fancies with glorious grace.
The cravings adorned, they fit like a glove,
Whispering secrets that sparkle with love.

The Art of Desire

In corners of closets where shadows delight,
Hang garments adorned, shimmering bright.
A bow tie's a joker who knows all the gags,
While trousers ponder life, in splendid rags.

A dress with a flair, it sways and it swirls,
Inviting the dance with mischievous twirls.
The suspenders giggle, while socks play with fate,
Unruly companions who can't seem to wait.

With pockets of sunshine, oh what a surprise,
They store all the giggles and sweet little lies.
Who knew that a shirt could be so coy and fun?
Each sleeve hides a smile, each seam is a pun.

So here's to the pieces that tease and that play,
A tapestry woven in a comical way.
The art of affection sewn tight in our style,
With chuckles and charms that together can pile.

Chasing Shadows in Fabric

Through shadows of curtains, where splashes of light,
Create outfits of fancy that giggle with might.
A bowler hat teeters, now isn't that bright?
A mustache on pants does a jig, what a sight!

Shirts wear puns proudly, as collars salute,
Each button a bard, reciting its route.
Dresses aspire, to pick up the pace,
While shoes join the fun, setting forth on their chase.

With fabric that flutters like butterflies bold,
Each twist brings a tale just waiting to unfold.
Scarves slip and slide, and what do they find?
A ribbon that tickles the humor entwined.

So let's spin a yarn with our patterned parade,
As laughter and fashion in chaos cascade.
In the chase for the shadows, we embrace the jest,
A whimsical dance in the fabric's own quest.

Silken Threads of Reminiscence

In a drawer, so sweetly hid,
A tangled mess, of things we did.
Naps taken on a sunny floor,
Forgotten dreams we can't ignore.

The mismatched socks, oh what a pair,
They dance around, without a care.
They tell tales of mishaps grand,
A sock puppet show, unplanned!

Giggles echo in the night,
As shadows stretch and take to flight.
With cherry pie upon the sill,
We spin our fables, what a thrill!

Inloophole mysteries we confide,
A tangled heart we tried to hide.
We laugh at rhymes, a silly spree,
These threads of joy, they set us free.

Entangled Aspirations

With every wish on paper planes,
We soar, despite the silly chains.
A kite on strings, it dips and dives,
We laugh at all our dreams' archives.

A shoelace twist, a double knot,
A tangled tale in quite a spot.
We chase ambitions, wild and bold,
While growing older, never old!

In the kitchen, pots collide,
We cook up dreams and let them ride.
With spoons as wands, we sprinkle cheer,
And serve our hopes right here, my dear!

So here's to goals we sometimes miss,
Each failure wrapped in giggles and bliss.
With every fumble, every cheer,
The dance of life is crystal clear.

Patterns of the Heart

In every quilt, a story's spun,
Each patch a dream, a little fun.
With buttons lost and seams undone,
We stitch our joys 'til day is done.

A coffee cup that spilled and splashed,
The morning rush, we laughed and dashed.
With all our patterns, bold and bright,
We weave a tale of pure delight.

A heart-shaped cookie, oh so sweet,
Dancing crumbs beneath our feet.
Chasing laughter, catching sighs,
In silly hopes, our love complies.

On paper hearts we scribble dreams,
In glitter glue, our laughter gleams.
With every stitch and the thread we part,
We find the joy in every heart.

Nuances of Nostalgia

Remember when we raced the breeze?
In shirts too big, we climbed to tease.
With crayons wild, we drew the sky,
   And made the clouds our alibi.

Old photos flit like fireflies,
With goofy grins and bright blue eyes.
Each snapshot shaking, giggling so,
   Our little secrets glimmered low.

In forgotten hats, we find our flair,
A silly dance beyond compare.
With mismatched shoes, we twirl and spin,
   In this mad world, we dive right in.

From silly songs to awkward teens,
Our history's just bursting seams.
Each memory a joyful jab,
   In laughter's quilt, we still can fab!

www.ingramcontent.com/pod-product-compliance
Lightning Source LLC
Chambersburg PA
CBHW062109280426
43661CB00086B/396